STEP BY STEP

A linked series of Board Books, Concept Books and Story Books
for the pre-school child

Board Books	*Concept Books*	*Story Books*
My House	Colours	Wet Paint
Day Time	Counting	Down in the Shed
Night Time	Noises	Over the Wall
Shopping	Big and Little	There and Back Again

First published 1988
by William Collins Sons & Co Ltd
in association with The Albion Press Ltd

© text Diane Wilmer 1988
© illustrations Nicola Smee 1988

British Library Cataloguing in Publication Data
Wilmer, Diane
Wet paint. — (Step-by-step).
1. Readers — 1950–
I. Title   II. Smee, Nicola   III. Series
428.6   PE1119

ISBN 0-00-181123-1

Printed and bound in Hong Kong by South China Printing Co

STEP BY STEP

Wet Paint

Diane Wilmer
illustrated by Nicola Smee

COLLINS
in association with THE ALBION PRESS

When Nicky and Mum finished
painting their front door it looked lovely.
"Painting is fun!" said Nicky.
"Let's do it again."
"No," said Mum.
"We must leave it to dry."

But everybody wanted to use the door,
even when it was still wet.

So Nicky found his chalks and
he and Mum wrote
WET PAINT
all over the doorstep and the wall.

But nobody took any notice.

WET PAINT

The postman came striding down the
path and was just about to shove
some letters through the letter-box
when Nicky spotted him and yelled –
"No! Look! WET PAINT."

Dan didn't see Nicky's writing either.
"Don't touch the door!"
yelled Nicky.
"WET PAINT!"

"Oh no," said Dan.
"Have I got it on my tracksuit?"

Then Mrs Wood came round.
Nicky just stopped her from knocking
on the front door.

"Look!" he yelled. "WET PAINT!"

"What is the matter with everybody?"
moaned Nicky.
"Can't they read?"

He wrote
WET PAINT
all over the place and drew an arrow
on the pavement so that people would
go round the back.

It did the trick.
Everybody went round the back.

wet
paint

Everybody except Kit and Jack.
They loved to curl up on the
doorstep in the sun but
it was usually far too busy.
Now it was just perfect.
They stayed there all afternoon.

wet

The next morning Nicky rubbed out all his writing and his arrow.

"Now people can knock at our shiny front door," he said.

They all came –
the postman and
the paper girl,

Mrs Wood,

Dan,

Clare and Dad.

RAT-A-TAT-TAT

It was Mum who saw the marks
on the bottom of the door.
"What are these?" she said.
Nicky looked at Kit's paws.
Her front ones were yellow.
He looked at Jack's paws.
They were yellow too.

"They're covered in paint!"
said Mum.
"It's not their fault,"
said Nicky.
"They can't read."
"Well, that's a pity," said Mum.
"Now we'll have to paint the
door all over again."
"Yippee!" shouted Nicky.
"Painting is fun!"